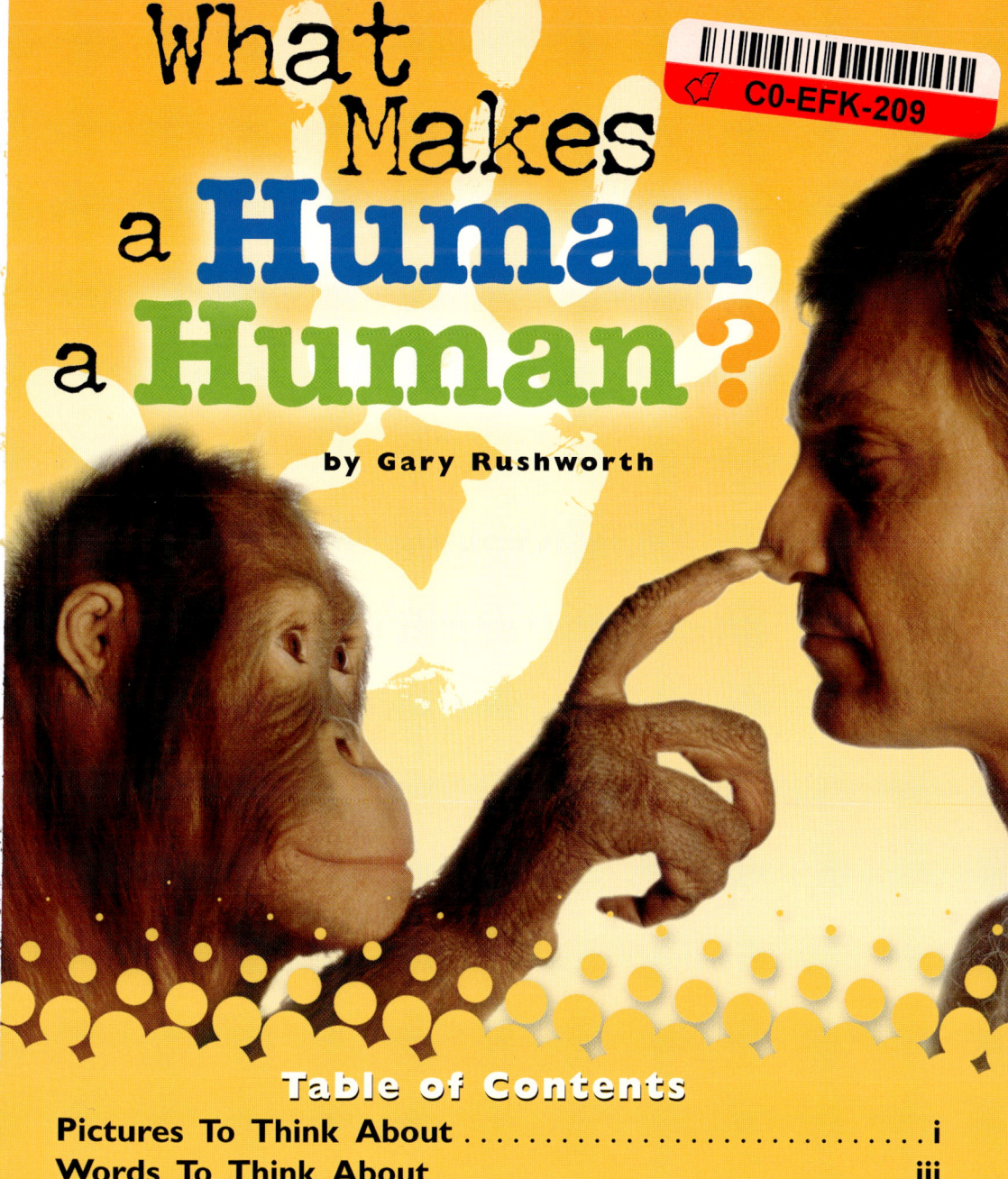

What Makes a Human a Human?

by Gary Rushworth

Table of Contents

Pictures To Think About i
Words To Think About iii
Introduction 2
Chapter 1 • What Makes Us Human? 4
Chapter 2 • What Makes Humans
            Alike and Different? 14
Chapter 3 • What Do Humans Need to Survive? 20
Conclusion 28
Glossary 31
Index 32

Pictures To Think About

mitochondria
cell membrane
ribosomes
nucleus

What Makes a Human a Human?

Words To Think About

Characteristics
- passed down from parents
- affects how we look or act
- ?

Examples
- eye color
- hair color
- ?

trait

What do you think the word **trait** means?

Homo sapiens

What do you think the term *Homo sapiens* means?

Latin: homo (human being)

Latin: sapiens (wise)

Read for More Clues
cell, page 17
Homo sapiens, page 5
trait, page 3

cell

What do you think the word **cell** means in this book?

Meaning 1
small room in a jail (noun)

Meaning 2
basic building block of all living things (noun)

Meaning 3
small group of a political party (noun)

iv

Introduction

Earth has billions of animals. Some animals are big. Some animals are small. Some animals are humans. That is right! Humans are a type of animal. Do you know why?

▲ People and animals are related.

This book is about humans. In this book, you will see how humans have changed over time. You will learn about **traits** (TRAYTS), or characteristics. You will find out what traits make humans special.

Read on. Find out what makes a human a human. Learn about—us!

CHAPTER 1

What Makes Us Human?

Earth has millions of different types of living things. It is hard to keep track of them all. Scientists thought of a way to help. Scientists classify, or sort, living things into groups. The living things in each group have common traits. This way of sorting is called classification (kla-suh-fuh-KAY-shun).

Careers Anthropologist

Anthropology is the study of human beings. An anthropologist studies fossils, ancient bones, and artifacts. They learn about what life was like long ago. Fossils help them see how different organisms lived. Would you like to be an anthropologist? You need to study science and history. Most anthropologists go to graduate school after college.

A **kingdom** (KING-dum) is the biggest group. All plants are in the plant kingdom. All animals are in the animal kingdom.

Inside each kingdom are levels of smaller groups. These smaller groups sort things further. The **species** (SPEE-sheez) level has the smallest groups. Animals in a species are all the same. For example, all humans are the same species.

▲ Humans are *Homo sapiens* (HOH-moh SAY-pee-enz). *Homo sapien* means "the wise or clever human." *Homo sapiens* are the only human species that are still alive.

CHAPTER 1

Think about humans and dogs. How are they alike? Both are types of animals. That means humans and dogs are in the same kingdom. Humans and dogs have backbones. That means they are in the same phylum (FY-lum). In both groups, babies drink milk from their mothers. That means humans and dogs are in the same class, too.

Humans and dogs also have many differences. People stand up straight and walk on two legs. Dogs walk on all four legs. Many animals walk on four legs. Many other animals, like snakes, have no legs at all. Walking on two legs makes humans special.

Everyday Science

A man named Carolus Linnaeus created the classification system that is still used today. He called humans *Homo*. *Homo* comes from the Latin word meaning "person."

WHAT MAKES US HUMAN?

At first, classification had only two kingdoms. They were the plant and animal kingdoms. Each kingdom had two groups inside. The groups were the **genus** (JEE-nus) and the species. A genus is a larger group than the species.

Over the years, people added more groups. Today, we have five kingdoms. Inside each kingdom are six levels of groups. Look at the chart below. You can see the levels of groups.

Classification

Kingdom	Animalia	Large group of organisms comprising only animals
Phylum	Chordata	Animals that have a spinal cord
Class	Mammalia	Animals that feed milk to their young
Order	Primates	Highest order of primates (human, gorilla, monkey)
Family	Hominidae	Animals that walk on two legs
Genus	*Homo*	Humans
Species	*Homo sapiens*	Modern man

CHAPTER 1

The Beginning of Man

Humans have lived for millions of years. Over time, humans have changed. The first people were shorter than people are today. They also had longer arms and legs than we do. Early humans learned to walk on two feet. Learning to walk on two feet changed how they lived. This meant that they could use their hands to gather food. They could also carry things. In time, they learned to make and use tools.

The Footprints

One important difference between humans and other animals is how people walk. In 1976, two scientists found a line of footprints in Africa. The footprints were more than 3.5 million years old. The footprints were in sand. A volcano erupted and covered the prints with ash. When it rained, the ash became as hard as cement. The footprints were proof that early humans walked on two feet.

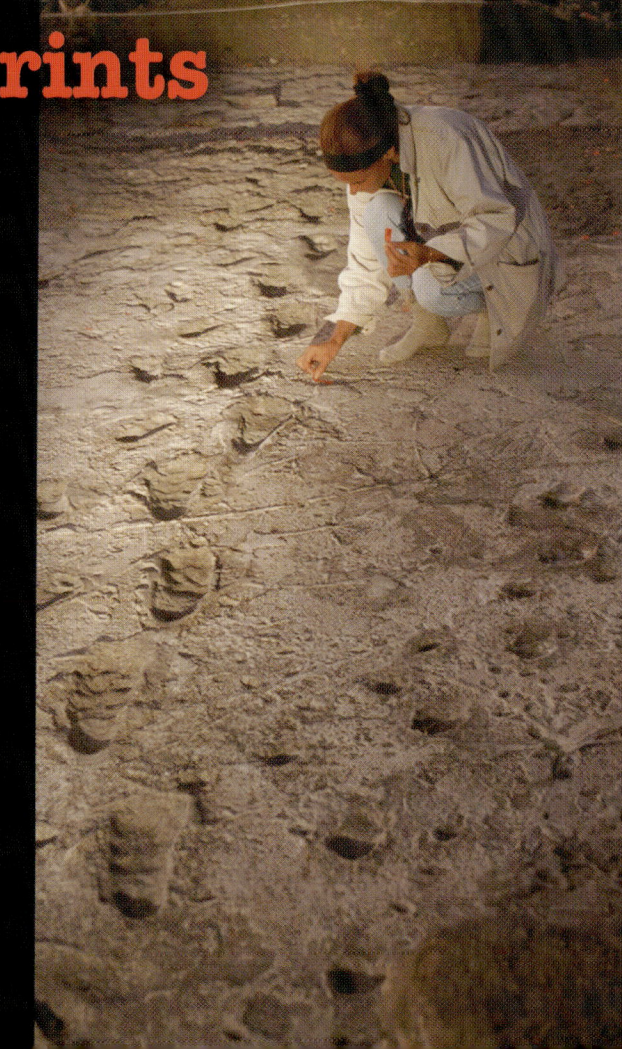

WHAT MAKES US HUMAN?

One example of an early human is Lucy. Lucy lived in eastern Africa. She lived more than three million years ago. In 1974, a scientist found bones in Africa. The bones were from a woman's skeleton. This skeleton was an early human. Scientists gave her the name Lucy.

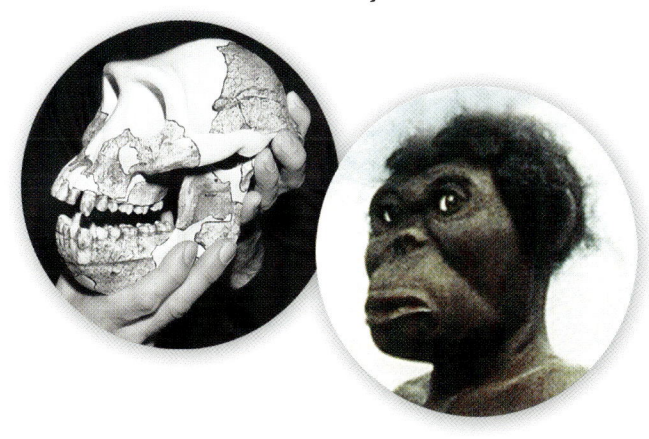

▲ Lucy was less than four feet tall. She walked upright, on two legs.

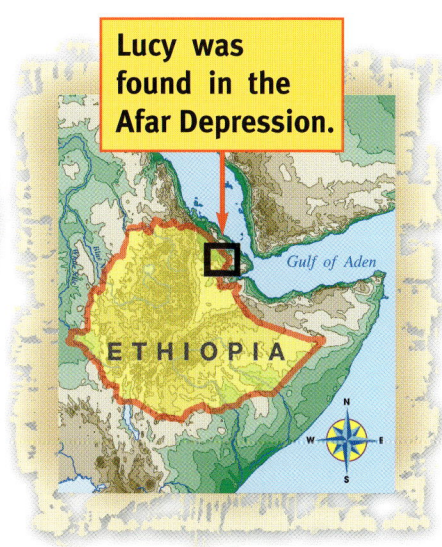

Lucy was found in the Afar Depression.

They Made a Difference

Mary Leakey is a famous anthropologist. She spent most of her life hunting for traces of early humans. Leakey first became famous for finding the skull of an early ape. The skull is more than twenty million years old. Only three other skulls like it have ever been found. Over her lifetime, Leakey worked hard to help people understand where they come from.

CHAPTER 1

Over time, humans began to **evolve** (ee-VAHLV), or change. One species of early man learned to make more tools. Then they learned to use fire to cook.

These people had bigger brains than the humans before them. These people were better thinkers.

Peking Man was a member of the *Homo erectus* species. Peking Man lived in China. He lived between 250,000 and 400,000 years ago. A scientist was working in China when a local man led him to Dragon Bone Hill. The hill was full of fossils. Between 1929 and 1937, the bones of forty humans were found. Then World War II started. The bones were to be sent to the U.S. for safety, but they disappeared on the trip. To this day, no one knows what happened to the bones of Peking Man.

WHAT MAKES US HUMAN?

Having fire meant people could live in colder places. People began to move to new places. Sometimes they followed the animals they hunted. One group of people learned to live in cold places. These people were short and stocky. Their small bodies helped them stay warm.

These people traveled together in groups. They formed communities. They took care of one another. They cared for sick people.

▼ Neanderthal (nee-AN-dur-thaul) men were about 5 feet 6 inches (1.68 meters) tall. Women were about 5 feet 2 inches (1.57 meters) tall.

✓ Point

Make Connections
The changes, or adaptations, in this chapter took many years. However, people also change in small ways every day. Think of a time you had to adapt to a new place or situation. What changed? How did adapting help you?

CHAPTER 1

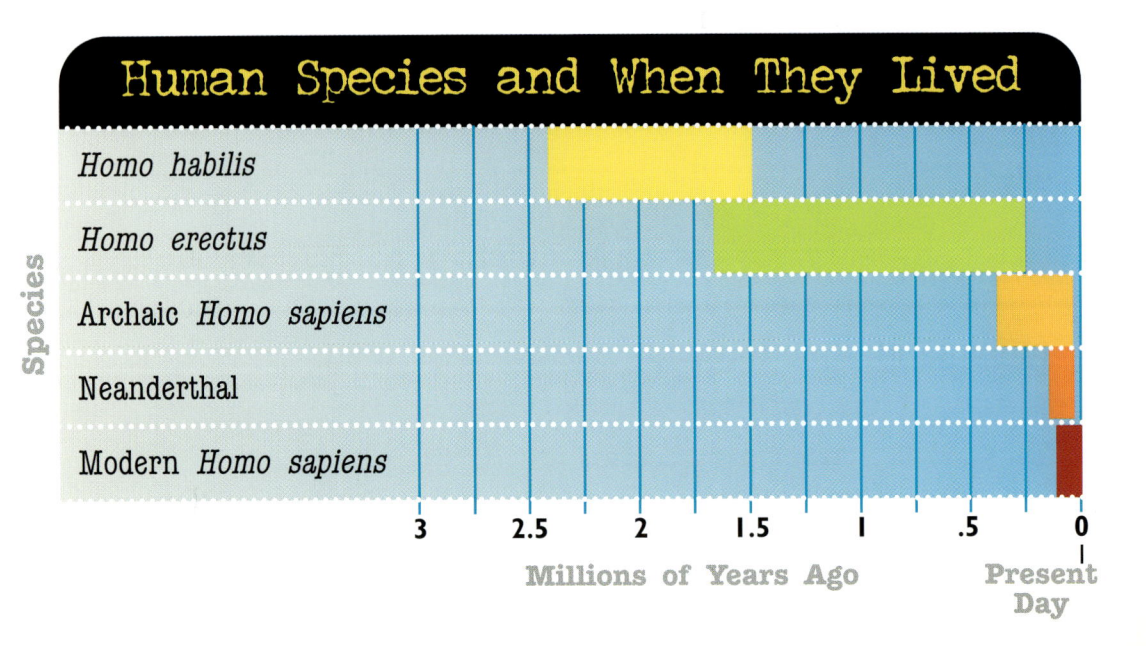

Human Species and When They Lived

Species	
Homo habilis	
Homo erectus	
Archaic *Homo sapiens*	
Neanderthal	
Modern *Homo sapiens*	

3   2.5   2   1.5   1   .5   0

Millions of Years Ago — Present Day

Some early species of man died out. No one knows why. But a new species took their place. The new species changed, or adapted, to the world around them. Those new people were a lot like people today.

Math Matters

It takes a lot of time for a new species to develop. The first ancestors of modern *Homo sapiens* developed over 14 million years ago. Modern *Homo sapiens* developed only about .1 million years ago.

WHAT MAKES US HUMAN?

How were these new people like us? Their brains were like ours. They could think and reason. They formed languages. They learned to solve problems. They also shared ideas.

Today, *Homo sapiens* have different names. We are called human beings, or people. We are also called humankind, the human race, or just man.

All humans are alike in some ways. People are different, too. People live in different places. People eat different foods. People speak different languages. People also have different traits.

▼ **Humans are social animals.**

CHAPTER 2

What Makes Humans Alike and Different?

Look at the people around you. What do you see? You know that they are humans. Some people you know. Other people are strangers. They are all part of the same species.

Humans have two eyes. Some eyes are brown. Some eyes are blue or green. Eye color is a trait. Traits are passed down by each parent. Each parent gets traits from his or her parents.

▶ People look the same in some ways, but they have differences, too.

Where Do Traits Come From?

Traits come from **DNA**. DNA is in our body. DNA carries information. DNA can show what a person will be like. DNA is what helps make each person special in his or her own way.

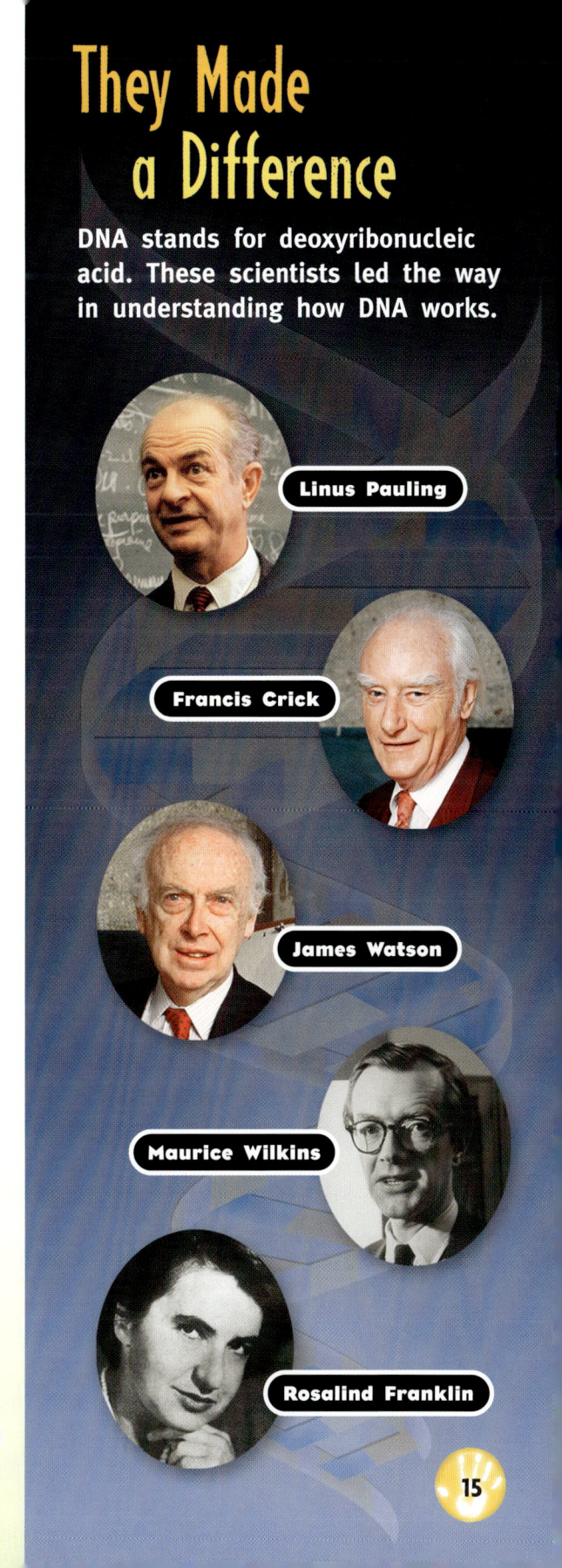

They Made a Difference

DNA stands for deoxyribonucleic acid. These scientists led the way in understanding how DNA works.

Linus Pauling

Francis Crick

James Watson

Maurice Wilkins

Rosalind Franklin

CHAPTER 2

What Is DNA?

DNA is a long chain of living material. Each chain of DNA has a pattern, or exact order, of chemicals. A DNA molecule looks like a twisted ladder.

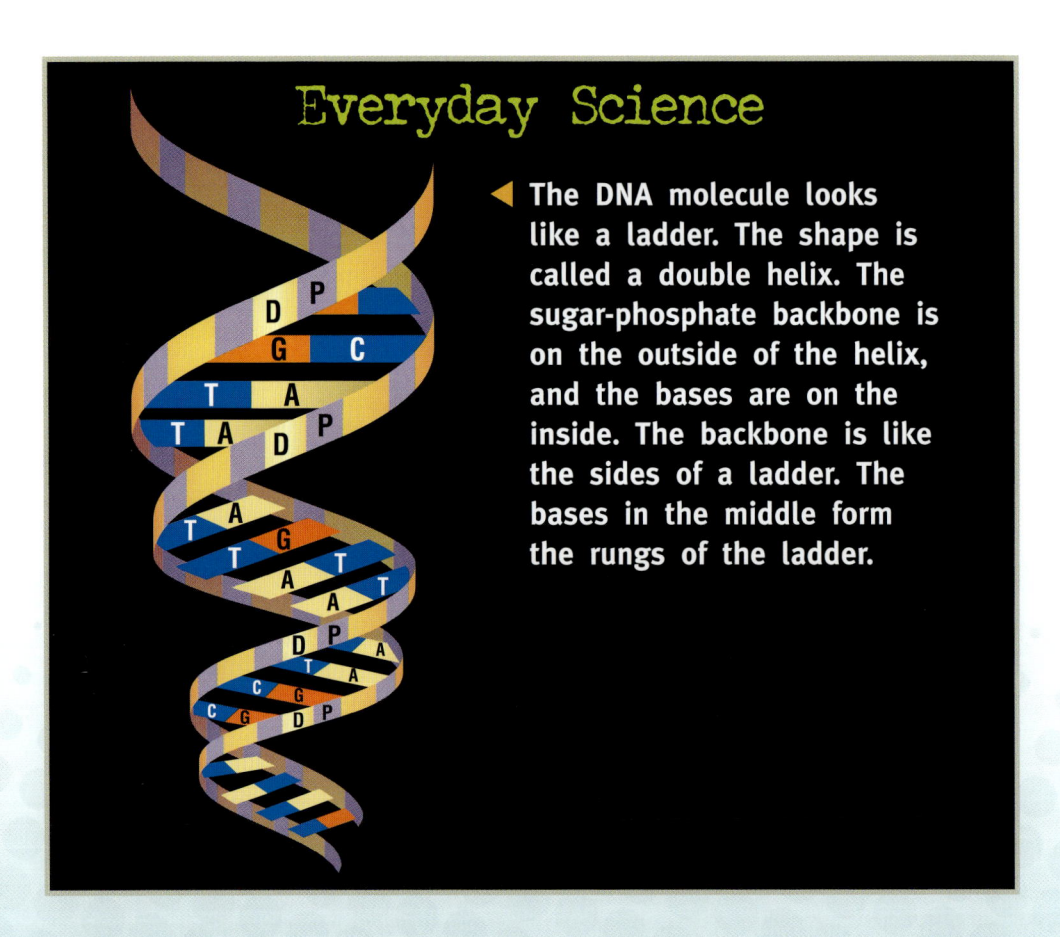

Everyday Science

◀ The DNA molecule looks like a ladder. The shape is called a double helix. The sugar-phosphate backbone is on the outside of the helix, and the bases are on the inside. The backbone is like the sides of a ladder. The bases in the middle form the rungs of the ladder.

DNA has the information needed to make a living thing. DNA also tells about our parents and their parents. This helps scientists learn about early humans. DNA helps scientists see how humans have changed.

WHAT MAKES HUMANS ALIKE AND DIFFERENT?

All living things have **cells** (SELZ). DNA is found in cells. Humans have billions of cells. Each cell has special parts. Each part has a different job.

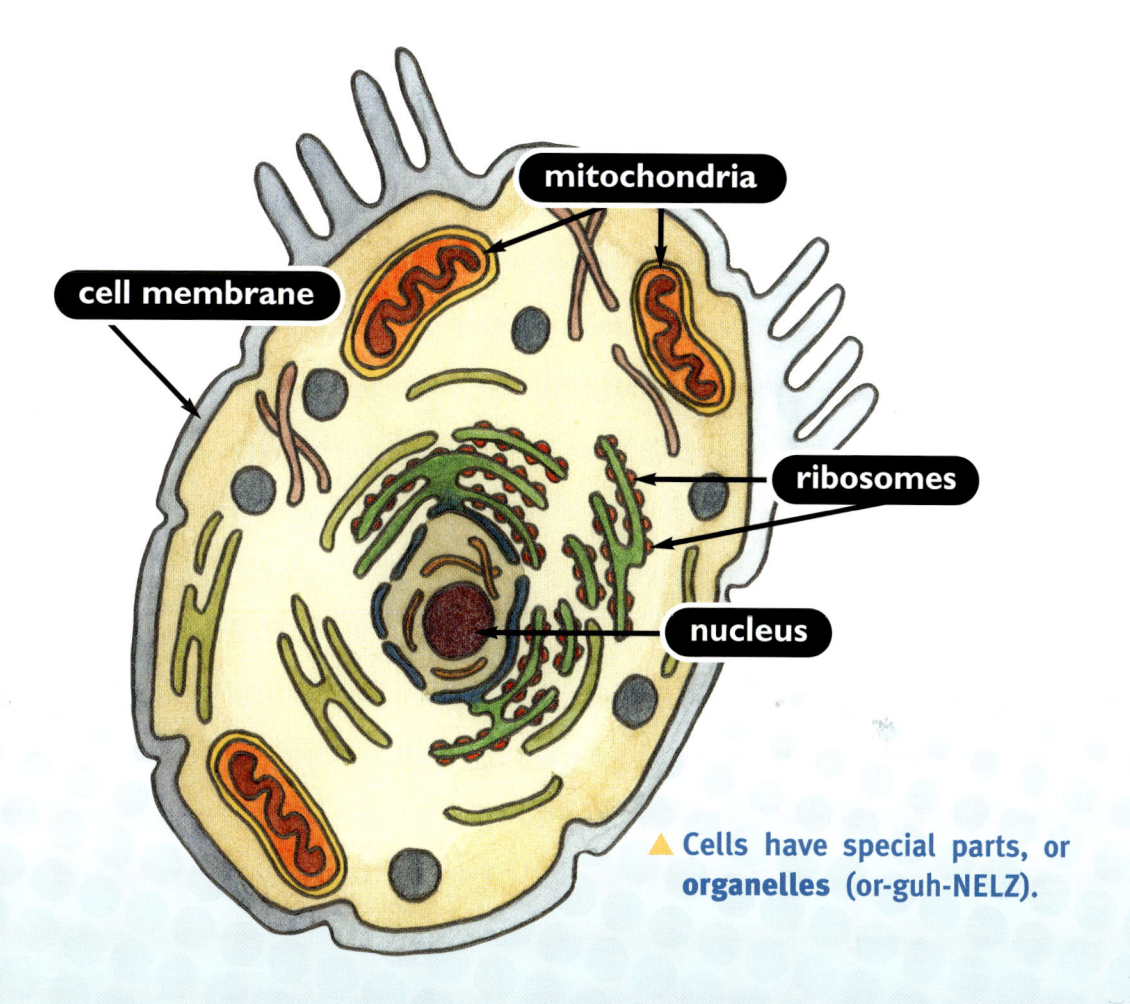

[Diagram labels: cell membrane, mitochondria, ribosomes, nucleus]

▲ Cells have special parts, or **organelles** (or-guh-NELZ).

One important part is the nucleus (NOO-klee-us). The nucleus is the brain of the cell.

Some other important parts are the **mitochondria** (my-toh-KAHN-dree-uh). These parts make energy for the cell.

CHAPTER 2

Each person gets DNA from each parent. You may have eyes like your mother's and hair like your father's. Your DNA is a mixture of both of your parents' DNA. Over time, a family's DNA changes.

One kind of DNA can only be passed from the mother. This DNA is passed on almost without change. Scientists study this DNA. They use it to learn about early humans. This special DNA is inside the mitochondria.

▲ Children inherit DNA from both their mother and their father.

It's a Fact

The study of DNA and heredity is called genetics.

WHAT MAKES HUMANS ALIKE AND DIFFERENT?

Mitochondrial Eve

Mitochondrial Eve was a female who lived in Africa more than 100,000 years ago. Scientists call her Eve because they believe she is the ancestor of all living humans. Beginning with Eve, each generation of her family had at least one daughter. These daughters continued to pass on their DNA. Today, ancestors of Eve live in every country in the world.

CHAPTER 3

What Do Humans Need to Survive?

All animals need basic things to survive, or stay alive. All animals need food. All animals need water, too.

The human body is 70% water. Humans cannot live without fresh water to drink. Water helps the body work. Water keeps the blood flowing. Water also helps get food to cells.

Food, clothing, and shelter are the basics of survival for humans.

Humans need food to make energy. Plants can make their own food. Humans cannot. People need a source of food to live. Humans eat plants and animals for food.

Early people gathered berries, nuts, and roots to eat. They drank water from rivers, streams, and springs. Over time, they learned to hunt for meat. They also learned to grow food.

▼ Early humans learned to hunt for food to survive.

CHAPTER 3

Clothing and shelter are other basic needs. Clothes were simple at first. Early humans used leaves and bark to make clothes. In hot places, few clothes were needed. As humans moved to colder places, they needed to stay warm and dry. Warmer clothes were made from animal skins.

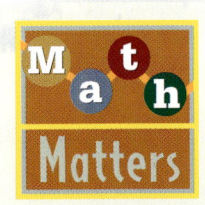

Math Matters

Humans are warm-blooded animals. Normal body temperature for a person is between 97–99 degrees Fahrenheit (36–37 degrees Celsius). If the body gets too hot—over 106°F (41°C)—cells can become damaged and may die. If the body gets too cold, body systems slow down and may even stop working.

Some early humans adapted to colder climates.

WHAT DO HUMANS NEED TO SURVIVE?

Early humans also needed shelter. In warm weather, they slept outside. Sometimes animals attacked them. So they found shelter in caves, or in trees. They also looked for high ground. There they could see if animals or other humans were going to attack.

Humans learned to make better tools. They began to build homes. They also made weapons for hunting and fighting. Soon, humans began to live and work together. In time, humans formed bonds with other humans. Slowly, communities formed.

As they developed, humans began to live together in small communities.

CHAPTER 3

When Life Changes

The first humans probably lived in Africa. Then they began to **migrate** (MY-grayt), or move. They moved to other areas. Why did they move? As humans changed, they were able to live in different places. Soon, people began to travel together.

Scientists study these moves. Scientists dig up tools. The tools show how humans lived long ago. Scientists have also found weapons. The weapons show that people fought wars. People probably moved often because of war.

Earth looked very different long ago. Earth had land in some places where there is now water. People walked great distances.

WHAT DO HUMANS NEED TO SURVIVE?

Human Migration

Scientists think that the earliest humans lived in Ethiopia. This country is in eastern Africa. From there, they moved to new lands.

Some humans moved to southern Africa. Others moved to what is now the Middle East.

Humans moved to Australia. Then they moved to Europe and Asia. Scientists learn how people moved by tracing DNA.

People in Africa today are related to people who moved to Asia long ago.

▲ **Scientists look for clues to the ancient past.**

CHAPTER 3

Human Migration

1. Scientists believe that the first descendants of modern humans lived about 200,000 years ago in Africa. That is where the oldest fossils have been found.

2. About 70,000 years ago, some humans migrated out of Africa. All modern humans that live in places other than Africa are descendants of those first travelers.

3. About 50,000 years ago, some humans left Africa for Asia. Scientists have found fossils of those people in Australia.

4. Early humans probably traveled through the Middle East to Europe about 40,000 years ago.

5. The people who traveled to Asia from Africa 40,000 years ago settled in what is now China, Japan, and Siberia.

6. Scientists do not know how humans first came to the Americas. Humans may have crossed from Siberia to Alaska about 15,000 years ago. At that time, the regions were connected by a land bridge. From Alaska, they probably traveled down the west coast to South America.

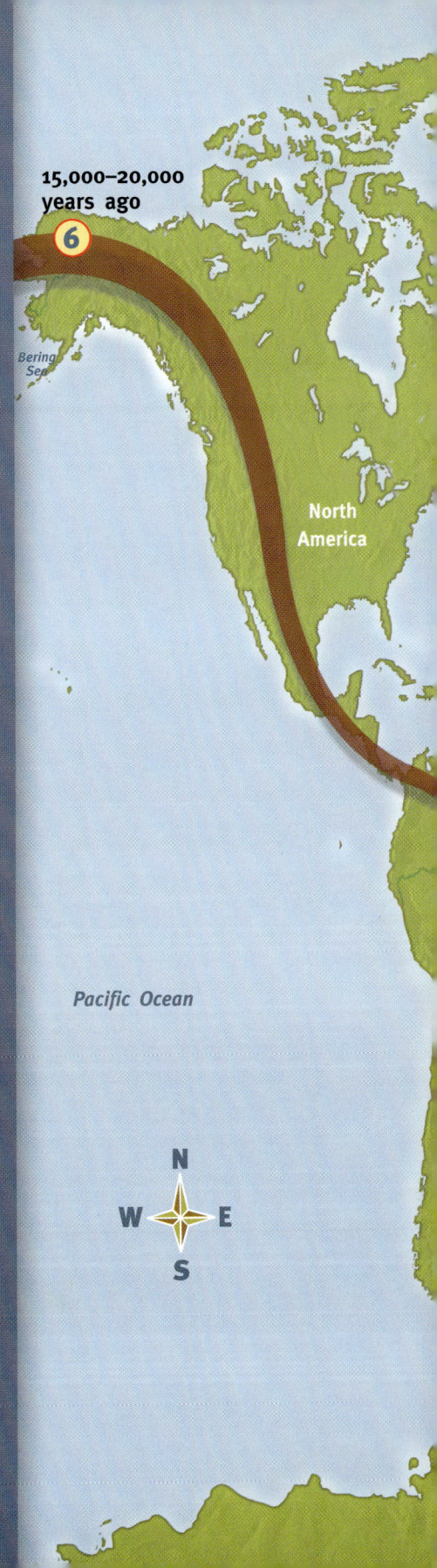

15,000–20,000 years ago

6

Bering Sea

North America

Pacific Ocean

WHAT DO HUMANS NEED TO SURVIVE?

Map labels:
- Arctic Ocean
- Atlantic Ocean
- Pacific Ocean
- Indian Ocean
- Southern Ocean
- Bering Sea
- Europe
- Africa
- Asia
- Australia
- South America
- Antarctica

Migration points:
1. 200,000 years ago — Omo Kibish, Ethiopia, oldest modern human
2. 50,000–70,000 years ago
3. 50,000 years ago (Australia)
4. 30,000–40,000 years ago (Europe)
5. 40,000 years ago
- 12,000–15,000 years ago

✓ Point

Reread

Make a list of all the countries mentioned in this book. Use self-stick notes to mark them on a wall map. Then use the map scale and a ruler to figure out how many miles humans traveled from place to place.

Conclusion

We have seen how living things are connected. We have learned how scientists keep track of living things. We have seen how humans are like other animals. We have seen how humans are different. We have learned how humans survive.

We owe a lot to the first humans. They learned how to stand up and walk. They gave us tools. They also learned how to make fire.

How are modern humans still like the first humans? How are we different? What traits help us survive?

CONCLUSION

Humans can think. Humans can reason and learn. Humans can build things. Humans can solve problems. Humans are curious. We can dream and create. These are some traits that make a human a human.

Glossary

cell   (SEL) the basic building block of an organism (page 17)

DNA   (DEE-EN-AY) a chemical that contains the genetic information of a cell (page 15)

evolve   (ee-VAHLV) the process of change related to evolution (page 10)

genus   (JEE-nus) a classification category (page 7)

Homo sapiens   (HOH-moh SAY-pee-enz) the genus and species to which humans belong (page 5)

kingdom   (KING-dum) a term used to classify different living things (page 5)

migrate   (MY-grayt) to move from one place to another (page 24)

mitochondria   (my-toh-KAHN-dree-uh) organelles found in a cell (page 17)

organelle   (or-guh-NEL) a part of a cell (page 17)

species   (SPEE-sheez) a term used to classify living things that are alike (page 5)

trait   (TRAYT) a characteristic that is inherited, or passed down, from generation to generation (page 3)

Index

cell, 17, 20

class, 6–7

DNA, 15–19, 25

evolve, 10

genus, 7

Homo sapiens, 5, 7, 12–13

kingdom, 5–7

migrate, 24, 26

mitochondria, 17–19

organelle, 17

phylum, 6–7

species, 5, 7, 10, 12, 14

trait, 3, 13–15, 29–30